# Animal Fair

poems by Amy Danforth
drawings by Susan Sturgill

CRICKET PUBLICATIONS

P.O. Box 8771     Toledo, Ohio 43623

**Animal Fair**

Poems copyright © 1983 by Amy Danforth
Drawings copyright © 1983 by Susan Sturgill

**ISBN** 0-912883-00-6

To Steve — For all your love and support

-and-

To Panos — The flame that lit the fire

## WHAT'S THE WORLD COMING TO?

Oh, the strange folks that you meet
As you walk on down the street.
Don't you wonder, as I do,
What the world is coming to?

# THE RABBIT BAND

They play country, blues, and jazz;
Lots of other razz-mi-tazz.
They give every song pizzazz.
They're the Rabbit Band.

Clarinet and trombone, too;
Oh, the music they can do.
And they'll play their best for you.
They're the Rabbit Band.

They will practice day and night.
Everyone must play just right.
Each new song is a delight.
They're the Rabbit Band.

They have traveled far and wide,
All across the countryside,
Playing songs by Charley Pride.
They're the Rabbit Band.

People come from far and near —
They love music, that is clear.
Take a seat and lend an ear.
They're the Rabbit Band.

## GOOD TO EAT? I WOULDN'T KNOW.

There ought to be some kind of law
About the way they package food.
For nothing makes me more upset,
Or puts me in the blackest mood,
Than when I'm hungry, but can't eat,
Because the wrapper's fastened tight.
So in frustration I give up —
Who wants to eat a scrawny knight?

# PIG OF MY HEART

All my heart I'll give to you
And my extra meal scraps, too,
If you will but be my bride
And alone with me abide.

Share with me my humble sty
And in gooey mud we'll lie,
Side by side contentedly,
If you will but marry me.

From your back I'll chase the flies,
While I gaze into your eyes.
And in time our home will fill
With small piglets eating swill.

Just to you I'll sing of love,
Sitting 'neath the moon above.
Promise me you'll be my wife —
Come, sweet sow, and share my life.

## THE BICKERSONS

The Bickersons squibble and squabble and squawk
And snicker and snigger whenever they talk.
They constantly argue and quarrel and fight,
Each one believing that his view is so right.
They badger, they needle, they screech, and they scream.
They can not converse without making a scene.
There's only one way you can make yourself heard —
Tape shut their big mouths so they can't say a word!

# TURTLE'S SOUP

First you'll need some stagnant water,
And be sure it has green slime,
Bring it to the point of boiling
Then add just a pinch of thyme.
Next, toss in some chopped up carrots,
Onions, and sliced mushrooms, too.
Then, stir in one cup of beetles —
Any type and size will do.
To this mixture add some minnows,
Three or four, if not too small,
And two cups of mashed mosquitos,
Wings and legs and heads and all.
Cream together twelve black spiders
With one cup of honey-bees.
Add to this three big fat earthworms
And one pint of powdered fleas.
In the pot, now, pour this mixture,
Season with some herbs and spice.
Simmer gently for one hour—
You will find this soup quite nice.

# A COOL VIEW

In summer I like to be lazy —
Just sit on my porch and drink tea.
Some people will say that I'm crazy
And think something's odd about me.
But, really the others are foolish —
They don't have the sense of a gnat.
I'd much rather be where it's coolish —
Now, what is so strange about that?

# WHERE DO BABIES COME FROM?

Everybody knows that babies
Under cabbage leaves don't grow.
Nor does dear old Santa bring them,
Though there's some that think it's so.
Little elves do not produce them,
Fairies are not in that trade,
Gypsies do not steal and sell them,
Not by magic are they made.
Babies are not found on doorsteps,
Hospitals don't give them out,
Doctors, in their bags, don't bring them,
Not in gardens do they sprout.
Oh, they say a gal named Venus
Drifted in upon a shell.
There are other tales we've heard of —
But these myths are hard to quell.
No, the facts are plain and simple —
Storks bring babies. Yes, it's true.
All along you knew the answer
To this question, didn't you?

# CROC POT

Some folks have bathtubs and nice showers and such,
And saunas and whirlpools, too.
But I am unique and, therefore, as you see,
The regular just won't do.

I looked high and low until, at long last,
I found the best tub there can be —
You just plug it in and turn on the switch.
The croc pot is perfect for me!

# PIGGING OUT

We're sick of people telling us
That being fat is out.
We simply fail to understand
What all the flap's about.

An architect there never was
Who made a better feast.
And calories, cholesterol
Concern us not the least.

Each roll of fat and double chin
We show with pride and glee.
It's clear a day has not passed by
Where we have gone hungry.

Some folks will say we're gluttonous,
Obese, and hoggish, too.
We like to think we're gourmands and
Leave rabbit food to you.

## SLEEPING OUT

I like to sleep beneath the stars
With leafy trees above my head.
With cookies, milk, a book, my bear,
Contentedly I go to bed.
The crickets sing a melody
With owls that chime in now and then.
They serenade to help me sleep —
I know I will come back again.

## BACHELOR BEARS

No one cares if clothes are dirty.
No one tells them what to eat.
Table manners are unheard of.
No one cares if they are neat.
Garbage pails can stay unemptied.
Bathroom sinks are a disgrace.
Things are seldom where they should be —
Nothing's in its proper place.
Dirty dishes don't offend them.
They get stacked up ceiling high.
And the oven door is perfect
If they have a shirt to dry.
All in all, these guys aren't fussy.
In fact, no one really cares,
Because life is lots of fun when
You can live like bachelor bears!

## THE VEGETABLE DRAGON

My mother says a dragon waits
To get small children, should they fail
To eat the things upon their plates —
She says this is no nursery tale.

My father says he knows of kids
Who did not eat their squash or beets.
The dragon came and ate them up,
While they were sitting at their seats.

I do not know if I believe
This story they are telling me.
But just in case it's true, I think
That I won't leave a single pea.

# MAGIC MIRROR

Magic Mirror, tell me true,
I've heard there's another who
Claims to be a beauty fair
With blue eyes and golden hair.

Yes, my lady, there is one
Who outshines the noon-day sun.
Gold beside her hair does pale
And she has the cutest tail.

Magic Mirror, tell me more
Of this pig whom I deplore.
Is she gentle? Is she sweet?
Is she dainty and petite?

Madam, though you stew and fret,
This Miss Piggy is no threat.
I don't think she's very smart —
To a frog she gives her heart.

Magic Mirror, can this be?
Surely you'd not lie to me.
Let Miss Piggy love green frogs —
I'll take care of handsome hogs.

## I ASKED FOR IT

I've no one else to blame.
I should have kept my big mouth shut.
I said it all the same —
I wanted a large family.
This truely is absurd.
How did I know she really
Would take me at my word?

## THE ALLIGATOR SCARF DANCE

I know a sailor named Old Pete
That I had the chance to meet.
And for two days he told me tales
Of sea monsters, giant whales,
And awful storms and shipwrecks, too.
But the tale I have for you
Is of adventure and romance —
It's the Alligator Dance!

Pete's ship was wrecked, his mates all lost.
On an island he was tossed,
In a remote deserted spot
With days cool and nights so hot,
Where trees are pink and sand is green.
People there had not been seen
Until this sailor happened by,
When the moon was full and high.

So there he lay and was entranced
By the animals who danced
And spun and dipped and leaped and twirled.
All that night, they waltzed and whirled.
One pair stood out from all the rest,
And to Pete they seemed the best;
For all the others stepped aside.
From their midst this pair did glide.

Each had a scarf around him wrapped,
Waiving as they tipped and tapped.
And, arm in arm, they moved with grace
Toothy smiles upon their face.
Pete was enthralled, his eyes grew wide,
As the couple passed his side:
A dancing gator and gatee
That he never thought he'd see.

# ESKIMO CREAM PIE

Upon his plate they put a slice
Of Eskimo Cream Pie.
He licked his lips and drooled a bit
And gave a mighty sigh.

He eyed the crust and eyed the cream
And all that was between.
"To eat a slice of pie so rich
Has always been my dream."

So now without a further word,
Without another sigh,
He ate that slice, upon his plate,
Of Eskimo Cream Pie!

## THE SPIRIT OF PORKOPOLIS

When aviation was brand new,
There were so many people who
Thought that the airplane was a joke
And had no use for common folk.

But two young pilots made a boast —
They'd fly the mail from coast to coast.
In two days' time they'd make the flight —
With confidence they left that night.

Over the plains and fields they sped
And soon the mountains loomed ahead.
But then a storm began to brew —
Oh, would the pilots make it through?

The wind grew fierce and lightning flashed,
Their engine stalled, they almost crashed.
And hail came down as thunder boomed —
They thought for sure that they were doomed.

Across the mountains they did pray
For just one star to light their way.
The fuel tank was running low,
But still they had a ways to go.

The engine caught on fire and smoked —
Our heroes gagged and coughed and choked.
The smoke was thick, they could not see —
The very nearly topped a tree.

And then the aircraft pitched and rolled —
Their fast descent was not controlled.
The pilot fainted dead away —
Oh, could his partner save the day?

Without a single thought of fear,
He donned his aviator's gear,
Then calmly took the wheel in hand
And tried to find a place to land.

By now the night was fading fast —
The morning sun appeared at last.
Below them lay the landing field —
The crowd that gathered cheered and squealed.

The flight from Boston was complete —
Their mission was a daring feat.
And now, my friends, you know the tale
About the first flight of air mail.

# A PRINCELY LIFE

The prince, in regal fashion, rides
To find out where the dragon hides
And rescue maids, both young and fair,
That may be captured in its lair.

Oh, princes do so many things
To pass the time before they're kings.
I'm glad we still have princes who
Know all the things a prince must do.

# THE BELLE OF THE BALL

She has style, she has grace,
An aristocrat's face,
She is charming and stunningly tall.
Oh, her features are fine
And her dresses divine.
Yes, she is the Belle of the Ball.

All her jewels are rare,
She has gold, silken hair,
And her tales never fail to enthrall.
She is sweet and polite
And her wit a delight.
Yes, she is the Belle of the Ball.

She's demure and refined,
With a sensitive mind,
And all men in love with her fall.
She will put you at ease,
She is not one to tease.
Yes, she is the Belle of the Ball.

# KENTUCKY FRIED COLONEL

I wonder if the colonel's thought
What it is like to be a meal?
I doubt that he appreciates
Just how the chickens all must feel.
How would he like to be deep fried
And end up on a dinner plate?
I'm sure he would not be too thrilled
If extra crispy was his fate.
In fact, if all the roles were changed,
I'll bet his famous recipe
Would not be known at all because
He'd keep it in great secrecy.

# HIBERNATION

When the days are dark and dreary
And the cold north wind does blow,
Critters turn to hibernation
To escape the ice and snow.
Chipmunks stay in cozy burrows,
Bears find caves in which to sleep,
Squirrels, in their leafy nests lie,
When the snow is thick and deep.
In the mud banks by the rivers,
Turtles, crayfish, snakes, and toads
Tunnel down beneath the frostline,
Warm and safe in their abodes.
Beavers stay within their houses
When their ponds have turned to ice,
Foxes in their dens are resting,
Furry nests are fine for mice.
Frogs, however, are quite different
In the manner which they stay
Warm and comfy in the winter —
They rest in a grander way.
Sitting in their padded armchairs,
Feet propped up upon their stools,
Sipping brandy by the fireside —
They think all the rest are fools.
So the next time freezing weather
Is not fit for man or dogs,
Pity other woodland creatures —
Don't feel sorry for the frogs!

## CROSSTOWN BEAR

In the morning, right at nine,
At the bear stop is a line
Waiting for the crosstown bear —
Just one nickle is the fare.
Step right up and find a seat.
Please, no pushing. Watch your feet.
This one's full — no room to spare.
Catch another crosstown bear.

# THE TROUT QUINTET

Miss Pike sent us a lovely note
Inviting us for tea and cake.
The only problem is, you see,
Her home's the bottom of a lake.

"I know you can not stay for long
And you will get a trifle wet,"
Her note explained and then went on,
"But you must hear the Trout Quintet."

"They've just arrived from Neptune's court,
Where they did play most splendidly,
And I was happy that they'd come
To play some music for my tea."

And so we went to Miss Pike's home
And, yes, we got a trifle wet.
But it was worth it just to hear
The music of the Trout Quintet.

## BATHING BEAR

Do you wonder just how a polar bear keeps
His fur coat so clean and so white?
He uses warm water and plenty of soap
And puts them to use every night.

If you should think that I am making this up,
I beg you to ask any bear.
He'll say, "In the Artic, I must take a bath —
There aren't any dry cleaners there."

# FROG LEGS

Every time that you eat frog legs,
You should feel so very bad,
Because, though you may not know it,
You have made a poor frog sad.

Just imagine, for a moment,
That you had no legs at all,
Because someone chose to eat them —
Now you'd have to creep and crawl.

Happily, there is a restaurant
Where these legless frogs can go,
And they get what they go in for
Without spending lots of dough.

Andy Pasto's making millions,
Not because his pasta's good,
But because he carries frog legs,
Which provides his livelihood.

Andy caters to his clients
And they leave most satisfied —
In they come with downcast faces,
Out they go with jumpy stride.

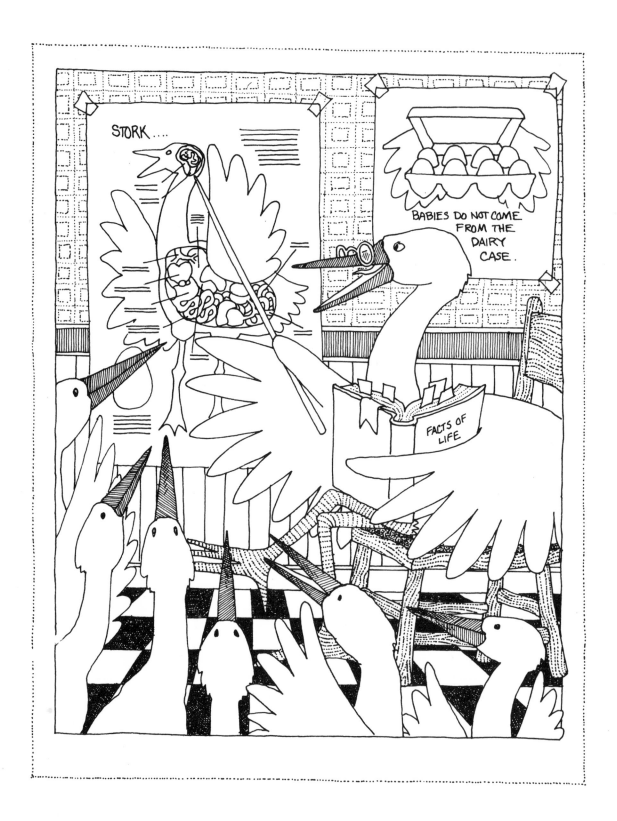

52

## WHICH CAME FIRST?

Authorities, throughout the years,
Have oft debated which came first —
The chicken or the lowly egg?
And though these men are very versed,
The question still remains unsolved:
It seems nobody can agree
On which came first and which came last —
They'll argue 'till infinity.
We birds have always known the truth
And we could set the record straight.
But, since no one has asked us yet,
The answer we will not relate.

# THE ROYAL MEAL

"His Majesty, the King, would like
A feast prepared today."
The page informed the palace chef,
"Please start it right away."

And so the chef began to plan —
Each dish a new delight;
He worked and fixed and shaped and fussed
Until they looked just right.

The banquet hall was all set up;
The table now was spread.
The King came in and sat right down
Directly at its head.

The chef came out and asked the King,
"Is everything all right?"
The King replied, "Oh, yes, indeed.
This is a royal sight."

But then there came a buzzing sound
Above his golden chair;
They looked and found a big, black fly
That darted through the air.

The King put down his royal fork —
A gleam came in his eye —
He asked the chef, "If you don't mind,
I'd rather have the fly!"

# THE OTHER WAY AROUND

I wonder if I'd think it fun
To swim around and splash about,
When if, instead of looking in,
I was inside and looking out!

# INDEX

Amy Danforth lives in Toledo, Ohio with her husband, Steve, and infant son, Justin. After six years of teaching elementary school, she retired to devote more time to writing children's books and gardening. She especially enjoys lyrical verse because, "It's fun to write."

Susan Sturgill was born in North Carolina, studied art at Rhode Island School of Design and currently lives in Cincinnati. She is an etcher, a drawer of jigsaw puzzles and an illustrator of books (two so far). She works with funny stories about animals because animals are easier to draw than people.